T0354476

This journal belongs to

_____

A Conversation with My Soul

A Walk to Your Soul

From My Heart to Yours

Dixie Daly

BALBOA
PRESS

A DIVISION OF HAY HOUSE

Balboa Press books may be ordered through booksellers or by contacting:

Balboa Press
A Division of Hay House
1663 Liberty Drive
Bloomington, IN 47403
www.balboapress.com
1 (877) 407-4847

Print information available on the last page.

ISBN: 978-1-5043-9973-9 (sc)
ISBN: 978-1-9822-0005-3 (e)

Balboa Press rev. date: 09/11/2018

A Conversation with My Soul: A Walk to Your Soul

From My Heart to Yours is dedicated to my beloved Husband and best friend Ed: An amazing husband, father, brother, uncle, Pop-Pop, and friend to many who knew him and didn't know him, whose love will live on forever and always! Amen

And my lovely granddaughters: Ashley, Alexa and Alyssa for their support in helping make this book come to life!

Their endless love they share with me is so precious. Reading and writing every quote and sharing such an experience with them will be remembered for the rest of their lives. Their future words of wisdom, that feed their own souls blossoms from this special experience. Nana says, Thank you.

When you live in gratitude and be grateful, your life will change right before your eyes. That's what my granddaughters did for me.

Credits:
Cover Designed by Phil Hansen
Cover Photo by Debbie Davis

Book edits by:
Judy Rethmeier
Kellyanne Zielinski
Lori Gama

These pages, in *"A Conversation with My Soul"* and *"A Walk to Your Soul,"* were created as a read it, write it, and journal it book.

From My Heart to Yours

A daily quote appears on each page to activate your thoughts and inspire you to open your heart, soul and mind.

Wake up your soul as you read these messages. Breath in each word, write it down, then share your thoughts of the day.

Part of the *wake-up-your-soul* process is in knowing and being clear by writing your thoughts down from your heart - first from your hand to paper - a valuable way to connect to YOU. May you bring joy and happiness to your life and realize you're in control of you!

It takes 21 days to change a habit. This 365-day journal will inspire you to be the difference in your life. It will motivate you to change your thoughts, to activate and to inspire you from within. What's nice about this journal, is that it starts when you're ready, which is any day of the year. In life all you have to do is Ask and then follow your heart.

Synopsis

What is Love? Love is a gift from God that we asked to experience here on earth. Love never fails or dies and will always survive because. God has given you more than enough to hold you through so much. You will think life will be perfect. What is perfect to you?

Faith is the key for all to see. Allow it into your heart and you will never be apart from the most precious gift of all.

The quotes you are about to read and experience through your own heart and soul will be life changing to let you learn, live, and let go of whatever is holding you back from the real you, that is to be simple and carefree.

The messages are meant to inspire us all to appreciate the wealth of life, especially the gift of love from our family and friends whom we are meant to observe while we're here to gain who we are.

There are messages to guide us, as long as we are silent enough to hear them.

The collection of quotes touches on topics that resonate with all readers, including faith, love, hope, grief, busyness, courage, strength, and to believe.

From the author:

If there is one thing I've learned on this earth, it is to know and understand that we hold our happiness key on what life is meant to be.

Please share *"A Conversation with My Soul": "A Walk to Your Soul"* *From My Heart to Yours with* someone dear to your own heart. Making a difference to encourage another human soul, will make the difference in you too. Writing *"A Conversation with My Soul"* *has been a healing process for me personally, who knew writing* *messages from God and creating a journal to share with the world* *was going to be part of a healing process and in finding myself again'*

Blessings,
Dixie Daly

Just Ask

Life is a Jouney for you and me
When we 'Just Ask' we are set free
It's plain and simple as can be
Just wait and you will see

Our guidance will guide us both day and night
Even when we don't know what's right
When you undecided which way to go
Remember all you have to do is 'Let Go'

Your answers are there when you walk
Shhh . . . Listen and let your guidance talk
When you 'Just Ask' then follow me
I will guide you to that place, Please believe in me

Life is a vessel inside of you
Embrace each moment because that's all you can do
Your passion will always be there for you to see
You must go within and bring it out for the world to see

Just remember ~ All you have to do Is 'Just Ask'

Your path is your journey
Designed with you in mind.
Now all you have to do
Is relax and let it unwind.

_____

_____

_____

_____

_____

_____

_____

_____

_____

_____

_____

_____

_____

_____

_____

_____

Seek for the goodness
In all you see.
Watch how life unfolds.
It's what you've always believed.

_____

_____

_____

_____

_____

_____

_____

_____

_____

_____

_____

_____

_____

_____

You have to step out of the box
To find yourself.
It's worth every move
To find you.

_____

_____

_____

_____

As we balance life,
We create more insight.

_____

_____

_____

_____

_____

_____

_____

_____

_____

_____

_____

_____

_____

_____

_____

_____

_____

The unknown lives
In your heart and soul
Just waiting to be told.

_____

_____

_____

_____

_____

_____

_____

_____

_____

_____

_____

_____

_____

_____

_____

_____

_____

Appreciation gives you
A perspective in life.

_____

_____

_____

_____

_____

_____

_____

_____

_____

_____

_____

_____

_____

_____

_____

_____

May the moonlight
Fill your heart tonight.

_____

_____

_____

_____

_____

_____

_____

_____

_____

_____

_____

_____

_____

_____

_____

_____

_____

_____

Give some love away;
More will come back to stay.

_____

_____

_____

_____

_____

_____

_____

_____

_____

_____

_____

_____

_____

_____

_____

_____

_____

Love is a miracle word
Giving you every reason to serve.

As you pray before
You fall asleep,
Be prepared to
Receive and repeat.

_____

_____

_____

_____

Clarity and focus
Will give you your desires.
Patience and time
Will let it be the test
To let it unwind.

_____

_____

_____

_____

_____

_____

_____

_____

_____

_____

_____

_____

_____

_____

_____

_____

_____

As you live your passion,
You will know your purpose.

_____

_____

_____

_____

As you walk on your path
Through your journey in life,
You will discover
More insight.

_____

_____

_____

_____

_____

_____

_____

_____

_____

_____

_____

_____

_____

_____

_____

_____

A breath of fresh air
Is like an open door
Allowing you to breathe in
And explore.

_____

_____

_____

_____

Combine your love and your faith;
Be ready for the open gates.

_____

_____

_____

_____

_____

_____

_____

_____

_____

_____

_____

_____

_____

_____

_____

You're a gift;
Live the presence.

_____

_____

_____

_____

Breathe in love.
Heaven is for real
And will not steal
Your love away.
It's just waiting
To give it back
To you to stay.

_____

_____

_____

_____

_____

_____

_____

_____

_____

_____

_____

_____

_____

_____

_____

_____

_____

Share the stories
Of your life
That bring back memories
To give you life.

_____

_____

_____

_____

_____

_____

_____

_____

_____

_____

_____

_____

_____

_____

_____

_____

Live your bliss;
Then receive pure happiness.

_____
_____
_____
_____

_____
_____
_____
_____
_____
_____
_____
_____
_____
_____
_____
_____
_____
_____

Open Your Heart

Open your heart
Love is so strong
Sometimes you just don't understand
What is in your plan

Open your heart
Make every day special and feel the love
You know it has been sent from up above

Open your heart
It was put there for you to have and to hold
Now all you have to do is embrace it with your soul

Open your heart
Because you will never feel apart
You see love is eternity for you to believe
Isn't that the way it was suppose to be

Open your heart
Because you're loved you so much
God is a moment away
From your every day
As you begin to pray

Information is ready
When you're ready for it.

_____

_____

_____

_____

_____

_____

_____

_____

_____

_____

_____

_____

_____

_____

_____

_____

_____

When in doubt,
Go to your heart.
The answers are there
Without a doubt.

_____

_____

_____

_____

_____

_____

_____

_____

_____

_____

_____

_____

_____

_____

_____

When life gets too busy
And steps in the way,
That's when it's time
To relax and play.

_____

_____

_____

_____

_____

_____

_____

_____

_____

_____

_____

_____

_____

_____

_____

_____

Capture in life
What you want to see in sight.
It's only a wish away
With love and pure light.

_____

_____

_____

_____

_____

_____

_____

_____

_____

_____

_____

_____

_____

_____

_____

_____

Conquer your fears
With faith and love here.

_____

_____

_____

_____

_____

_____

_____

_____

_____

_____

_____

_____

_____

_____

_____

_____

_____

_____

Love is . . .
Togetherness,
Forever being together.

_____

_____

_____

_____

_____

_____

_____

_____

_____

_____

_____

_____

_____

_____

_____

_____

_____

As the flowers bloom
For you,
It's to let you know
How special you are too.

_____

_____

_____

_____

_____

_____

_____

_____

_____

_____

_____

_____

_____

_____

_____

On Earth, you discover.
In heaven, you've been discovered.

_____

_____

_____

_____

_____

_____

_____

_____

_____

_____

_____

_____

_____

_____

_____

_____

We are here to discover new;
Begin by accepting you.

_____

_____

_____

_____

_____

_____

_____

_____

_____

_____

_____

_____

_____

_____

_____

_____

_____

Your many gifts
Are yours to be.
Just open your heart
And receive.

_____

_____

_____

_____

_____

_____

_____

_____

_____

_____

_____

_____

_____

_____

_____

Be blessed every day.
You get to share
Why you are here.

_____

_____

_____

_____

_____

_____

_____

_____

_____

_____

_____

_____

_____

_____

_____

_____

_____

_____

As you support
Someone's journey
To be new,
You're sharing
Part of you.

_____

_____

_____

_____

_____

_____

_____

_____

_____

_____

_____

_____

_____

_____

_____

Open your heart
And be a part
Of your life today.

_____

_____

_____

_____

_____

_____

_____

_____

_____

_____

_____

_____

_____

_____

_____

_____

_____

Start recognizing the people
In your life.
Watch everything
Change in sight.

_____

_____

_____

_____

Listen to the whispers
In your soul.
There are messages to be told.

_____

_____

_____

_____

_____

_____

_____

_____

_____

_____

_____

_____

_____

_____

_____

_____

_____

You can do
What you believe
To exceed and achieve.

_____

_____

_____

_____

_____

_____

_____

_____

_____

_____

_____

_____

_____

_____

_____

The one and only
Lives in your soul
Allowing you to live and let go.

_____

_____

_____

_____

_____

_____

_____

_____

_____

_____

_____

_____

_____

_____

_____

_____

_____

Ask for what you want;
Believe to receive.

_____

_____

_____

_____

_____

_____

_____

_____

_____

_____

_____

_____

_____

_____

_____

_____

_____

If you don't understand
Where somebody is at in life,
It's okay;
Embrace them anyway.

_____

_____

_____

_____

_____

_____

_____

_____

_____

_____

_____

_____

_____

_____

_____

_____

_____

_____

_____

Stay in the moment

Stay in the moment
Because it's all we have today
Your power is in the now
So go ahead and allow

Yesterday was yesterday
Tomorrow is not here yet
Today is a blessing

You must celebrate
To appreciate

Keep enthusiastic about life
Are you taking the wind out of your sail
Hoping you don't fail
Breathe a new life
Are you living or existing

Stay in the moment
It's worth every component
For you to have your wish
As you exist

Faith is what makes life
Transformational
And memorable.

_____

_____

_____

_____

_____

_____

_____

_____

_____

_____

_____

_____

_____

_____

_____

_____

_____

_____

As you turn the page
To another day,
You'll create memories to stay.

_____

_____

_____

_____

_____

_____

_____

_____

_____

_____

_____

_____

_____

_____

_____

_____

_____

_____

Hope. Love. Faith.
You have hope
As you have love
As you share faith.

_____

_____

_____

_____

_____

_____

_____

_____

_____

_____

_____

_____

_____

_____

_____

_____

To be loved . . .
To be listened to . . .
To be heard . . .
It's that simple.

_____

_____

_____

_____

_____

_____

_____

_____

_____

_____

_____

_____

_____

_____

_____

_____

_____

_____

Inspiration is what it takes
To have something new.
Be blessed
That it found you.

_____

_____

_____

_____

_____

_____

_____

_____

_____

_____

_____

_____

_____

_____

_____

_____

_____

Over the rainbow
There is light
To let you know
Everything is all right.

_____

_____

_____

_____

Life is like a Ferris wheel . . .
The circle of life
With ups and downs
With God in the center
Holding you together.

_____

_____

_____

_____

Everything in life
Is in the asking.
Create what you want to do
And watch it come through.

_____

_____

_____

_____

Life is a journey . . .
As you walk your path,
The outcome is revealed
Each moment of your dash.

_____

_____

_____

_____

_____

_____

_____

_____

_____

_____

_____

_____

_____

_____

_____

_____

_____

Walking in the light
Of fulfillment
Is living through
God in stillness.

_____

_____

_____

_____

Take care of everyone
Around you
And you'll be
Taken care of.

_____

_____

_____

_____

Be you . . .
That's all
You have to do.

_____

_____

_____

_____

_____

_____

_____

_____

_____

_____

_____

_____

_____

_____

_____

_____

_____

Once your soul
Understands love,
Gratitude and appreciation
Will be
All you can think of.

_____

_____

_____

_____

It doesn't matter
Who believes in you
As long as
You believe in you.

_____

_____

_____

_____

_____

_____

_____

_____

_____

_____

_____

_____

_____

_____

_____

_____

The center of love
Is the circle of life.

_____

_____

_____

_____

_____

_____

_____

_____

_____

_____

_____

_____

_____

_____

_____

_____

_____

_____

_____

Messages will come to you.
Listening to them
Will support
Your journey too.

_____

_____

_____

_____

_____

_____

_____

_____

_____

_____

_____

_____

_____

_____

_____

Happiness holds
The key to
Life's reality.

_____

_____

_____

_____

_____

_____

_____

_____

_____

_____

_____

_____

_____

_____

_____

_____

_____

Time is not given back.
Capture your moments
So they will last.

_____

_____

_____

_____

_____

_____

_____

_____

_____

_____

_____

_____

_____

_____

_____

_____

_____

A day of living
Is a day of giving
From your heart and soul.

_____

_____

_____

_____

_____

_____

_____

_____

_____

_____

_____

_____

_____

_____

_____

_____

The Path

Life is a journey right from the start
You just have to listen to your heart
Because it is deep within
That's where it begins

If you were once on the path
Wondering what to do
Know your guidance
Is there for you

Feel your emotions that's why they are there for you
Know God is always guiding you through and through
Because that is what he wants to do

The path to all greatness is something to understand
Because with God's grace we will all serve
And that's when it will hit a nerve

Joy and happiness will fill your heart
And really isn't that's what it's all about

The path is a journey from beginning to end
Go ahead and embrace the world today
Make a difference . . .

On your path today and give something away
You will change a life on the way
Because there is so much more that we can do
Please make a difference in someone's life to be new

Share your dream
With another human being.
Watch it come true
Because they have faith
In you.

_____

_____

_____

_____

_____

_____

_____

_____

_____

_____

_____

_____

_____

_____

_____

_____

_____

Love is . . .
Going out of your way
To make someone special today.

_____

_____

_____

_____

_____

_____

_____

_____

_____

_____

_____

_____

_____

_____

_____

_____

_____

_____

You hold your happiness key
On how you want
Life to be.

_____

_____

_____

_____

_____

_____

_____

_____

_____

_____

_____

_____

_____

_____

_____

_____

_____

_____

You're a magical being
Living a dream.

_____

_____

_____

_____

_____

_____

_____

_____

_____

_____

_____

_____

_____

_____

_____

_____

_____

_____

_____

You're never alone
With God in your soul
As he walks by your side
To let you get by.

      _____

      _____

      _____

      _____

_____

_____

_____

_____

_____

_____

_____

_____

_____

_____

Life is love
And love is life.
Whichever way
You look at it,
You're right!

_____

_____

_____

_____

_____

_____

_____

_____

_____

_____

_____

_____

_____

_____

_____

_____

_____

Give more
Than receive.
The key is
It's not from the same resource.

_____

_____

_____

_____

_____

_____

_____

_____

_____

_____

_____

_____

_____

_____

_____

_____

_____

Lessons in life
Are treated like
Another beginning of a day.
As you learn,
You'll be okay.

_____

_____

_____

_____

_____

_____

_____

_____

_____

_____

_____

_____

_____

_____

_____

_____

_____

As you open your heart,
The doors will open
For your day to start.
Be ready
To receive and believe.

_____

_____

_____

_____

_____

_____

_____

_____

_____

_____

_____

_____

_____

_____

_____

_____

_____

_____

Your heart holds a key
To see how special
You came to be.
Now unlock it
And you will see
God's plan for all to see.

_____

_____

_____

_____

_____

_____

_____

_____

_____

_____

_____

_____

_____

_____

_____

_____

_____

To have is to believe;
With prayer is to receive.

_____

_____

_____

_____

_____

_____

_____

_____

_____

_____

_____

_____

_____

_____

_____

_____

_____

_____

Blessings come every day.
Share your heart
And watch them stay.

_____

_____

_____

_____

_____

_____

_____

_____

_____

_____

_____

_____

_____

_____

_____

_____

_____

It's the details in life
That seem so small,
But it's the attention
You give them
That lets you have it all.

_____

_____

_____

_____

_____

_____

_____

_____

_____

_____

_____

_____

_____

_____

_____

God will always
Lead you
On your path
As long as
You leave the door open.

_____

_____

_____

_____

_____

_____

_____

_____

_____

_____

_____

_____

_____

_____

_____

_____

What you pray about
Think about
Comes about.

_____

_____

_____

_____

_____

_____

_____

_____

_____

_____

_____

_____

_____

_____

_____

_____

_____

Love everyone
You care about,
And care about
Everyone you love.

_____

_____

_____

_____

_____

_____

_____

_____

_____

_____

_____

_____

_____

_____

_____

_____

It's not about
The outside of us;
It's about
The inner soul
How life flows.

_____

_____

_____

_____

_____

_____

_____

_____

_____

_____

_____

_____

_____

_____

_____

Inspiring others in your life
Creates an energy
Of God in sight.

_____

_____

_____

_____

_____

_____

_____

_____

_____

_____

_____

_____

_____

_____

_____

_____

_____

Today choose love . . .
God's miracle gift
That unwraps from
Your heart and soul
With many blessings.

_____

_____

_____

_____

A Message from God

Listen to your heart and know
That you don't have to run anymore

A message from God
Just walk
To the Bible that is
Open it
Read a verse
Now converse
With your soul
Which you do hold

Now . . . ask a question
Then listen
For the answer
Now turn the page
There it is!
Right in front of you

Now put your hands together and pray
As we thank God everyday
And know that you don't have to run anymore
Just walk right into your soul

Isn't it nice to know
That you have the answers
Are within you from
A message from God

Every day you'll be walking a new path;
It's your journey to look at.
There will be many choices to make.
All you have to do
Is live in faith.

_____

_____

_____

_____

Your purpose lives within you
With so many things to do.
Living your passion every day
Brings out
Your purpose to stay.

_____

_____

_____

_____

_____

_____

_____

_____

_____

_____

_____

_____

_____

_____

_____

_____

Love yourself first
Before you give to anyone else.
You're a mirror of you
In everything you do.

_____

_____

_____

_____

_____

_____

_____

_____

_____

_____

_____

_____

_____

_____

_____

_____

Patience to the unknown
Is embracing the known.

_____

_____

_____

_____

_____

_____

_____

_____

_____

_____

_____

_____

_____

_____

_____

_____

Follow your heart . . .
It's where all the answers start.
The moment is living in the now,
The only time you have to allow.

_____

_____

_____

_____

Listening
Is not about
What's been said;
It's about
What is heard.

_____

_____

_____

_____

_____

_____

_____

_____

_____

_____

_____

_____

_____

_____

_____

_____

Living in the moment
Is your destiny
To your future.

_____

_____

_____

_____

_____

_____

_____

_____

_____

_____

_____

_____

_____

_____

_____

_____

_____

_____

There are days
Your heart will be tender,
Allowing you to stop in
With inspiration
From within.

_____

_____

_____

_____

_____

_____

_____

_____

_____

_____

_____

_____

_____

_____

_____

_____

_____

_____

_____

Life is a gift . . .
Certainly not to miss
The creativity in you
Making all of your dreams come true.

_____

_____

_____

_____

_____

_____

_____

_____

_____

_____

_____

_____

_____

_____

_____

_____

Change is something
That is put in front of you
Mainly to guide you
In a direction
You've never seen.
Be open
To receive and believe.

_____

_____

_____

_____

_____

_____

_____

_____

_____

_____

_____

_____

_____

_____

_____

_____

As God is guiding you
On your journey path,
He's giving you
So many blessings
For you to look at.

_____

_____

_____

_____

_____

_____

_____

_____

_____

_____

_____

_____

_____

_____

_____

_____

_____

_____

Let the branches in your soul
share a story that you hold.

_____

_____

_____

_____

_____

_____

_____

_____

_____

_____

_____

_____

_____

_____

God has big plans for you;
He's just waiting
For you to accept your gifts
With love and bliss.

_____

_____

_____

_____

In the mist of life
It might feel like a fog
Guiding you through
As your dreams are waiting for you.

_____

_____

_____

_____

_____

_____

_____

_____

_____

_____

_____

_____

_____

_____

_____

If you forgot to tell somebody
You love them,
It's not too late
If you're reading this.

_____

_____

_____

_____

_____

_____

_____

_____

_____

_____

_____

_____

_____

_____

_____

_____

Life is a journey . . .
Why not follow your path
And believe in all you can do;
That's what God has planned for you.

_____

_____

_____

_____

_____

_____

_____

_____

_____

_____

_____

_____

_____

_____

Positive thoughts allow
What you think about,
Comes about.

_____
_____

_____

_____

_____
_____
_____
_____
_____
_____
_____
_____
_____
_____
_____
_____
_____
_____

Brave you are;
Just reach
For the stars.

_____

_____

_____

_____

_____

_____

_____

_____

_____

_____

_____

_____

_____

_____

_____

_____

_____

Giving up on an
Opportunity-to-listen
Is giving up on an
Opportunity- to-share
Your love

_____

_____

_____

_____

_____

_____

_____

_____

_____

_____

_____

_____

_____

_____

_____

_____

The Key is Your key

I thought I had to buy a key
And realize it was inside of me

Just open up the treasure chest filled with love
You'll see the key sent from up above

It will open your heart
Now you know how it starts

God has your treasure waiting for you
Now you ask, What do I do?

Remember you hold the key
To see what it will be
When you look way out far
You'll see it in the stars

Now all you have to do
Is bring it into you

The key is your key
To your secret message
Waiting for you to open your heart
And listen

Because
That's all that you have been missing

Your personality is so real;
Don't let anyone steal
Who you are meant to be,
Amazing and carefree.

_____

_____

_____

_____

_____

_____

_____

_____

_____

_____

_____

_____

_____

_____

_____

_____

_____

_____

_____

_____

_____

Recognizing the change
That someone has made in your life
Will make the difference in you
In everything you do.

_____

_____

_____

_____

_____

_____

_____

_____

_____

_____

_____

_____

_____

_____

As you put energy in what you believe,
Be ready to create and receive.

_____

_____

_____

_____

Create the person you are supposed to be
With love and simplicity.

_____

_____

_____

_____

_____

_____

_____

_____

_____

_____

_____

_____

_____

_____

_____

_____

_____

Create more of who you are
By letting go
And reaching for the stars.

_____

_____

_____

_____

_____

_____

_____

_____

_____

_____

_____

_____

_____

_____

_____

_____

_____

A new day of change
To rearrange
Is a day of putting on your wings
And flying to your dreams.

_____

_____

_____

_____

_____

_____

_____

_____

_____

_____

_____

_____

_____

_____

_____

_____

God will put the right people
At the right time in your life
To give you strength and courage
To let you know everything will be all right.

_____

_____

_____

_____

_____

_____

_____

_____

_____

_____

_____

_____

_____

_____

_____

God is the key
As you walk through the fog.
He will guide you
Through it all.

_____

_____

_____

_____

_____

_____

_____

_____

_____

_____

_____

_____

_____

_____

_____

_____

_____

_____

Life lessons are only learned
When you walk into your future.
With one moment at a time,
You can watch them unwind.

_____

_____

_____

_____

_____

_____

_____

_____

_____

_____

_____

_____

_____

_____

_____

_____

Memories will play
In your heart every day,
Wanting to play
Over and over again
As you realize there is no end.

_____

_____

_____

_____

_____

_____

_____

_____

_____

_____

_____

_____

_____

_____

_____

What is your wish today?
Announce it;
Let it go.
It will show up in your life
Like a beautiful rainbow.

_____

_____

_____

_____

Inspiring others inside your life
Creates an energy of God in sight.

_____

_____

_____

_____

_____

_____

_____

_____

_____

_____

_____

_____

_____

_____

_____

_____

When you let go
And let God in control,
That's when your life unfolds.

_____

_____

_____

_____

_____

_____

_____

_____

_____

_____

_____

_____

_____

_____

_____

_____

_____

Everyone is at a different level of life.
Support them to be
For their future to see.

_____

_____

_____

_____

_____

_____

_____

_____

_____

_____

_____

_____

_____

_____

_____

_____

Lessons in life
Are treated like
Another beginning of a day.
As you learn, you will be okay.

_____

_____

_____

_____

_____

_____

_____

_____

_____

_____

_____

_____

_____

_____

_____

_____

_____

When your soul understands love,
Gratitude and appreciation
Will be all you can think of.

_____

_____

_____

_____

_____

_____

_____

_____

_____

_____

_____

_____

_____

_____

May your new year
Be so bright
And show you the light
For everything in sight.

_____

_____

_____

_____

Love starts with one heart;
Let it began with you
As you connect others too.

_____

_____

_____

_____

_____

_____

_____

_____

_____

_____

_____

_____

_____

_____

_____

_____

_____

Memories are created
Every moment of the day
Sealed in your heart
To forever stay.

_____

_____

_____

_____

_____

_____

_____

_____

_____

_____

_____

_____

_____

_____

_____

Believe in You

There is a reason you were put on this earth
To help the pain and the hurt

The message is clear
For all of us to hear
It's a message of love
Sent from God up above

It's so clear to see
That God wants us to believe
What you can be
For the world to see

All you have to do is plant a seed
Inside your heart
That's where it starts

It's your life you've been wanting to see
Remember, all you have to do is Believe!

Life is about
What you make it.
Believe in you
Is all you have to do.

_____

_____

_____

_____

Trust with patience;
Believe in the process
With faith.

_____

_____

_____

_____

Appreciate the moment;
It's your present,
For your tomorrow
Is such a gift.

_____

_____

_____

_____

_____

_____

_____

_____

_____

_____

_____

_____

_____

_____

_____

_____

Live your life
With love;
Walk your path
With faith.

_____

_____

_____

_____

Amazing as it may seem,
Everyone has
What it takes to believe.

_____

_____

_____

_____

_____

_____

_____

_____

_____

_____

_____

_____

_____

_____

_____

_____

_____

It's amazing how God
Brings opportunities
Into your life.
Recognizing them
Brings them to life.

_____

_____

_____

_____

_____

_____

_____

_____

_____

_____

_____

_____

_____

_____

_____

_____

What you focus on
You'll receive;
Focus on
What you believe.

_____

_____

_____

_____

_____

_____

_____

_____

_____

_____

_____

_____

_____

_____

_____

_____

_____

_____

Follow your heart . . .
It's where the answers start.

_____

_____

_____

_____

All you own
Is the present moment.
Feed it with a positive attitude
And you'll live
In much gratitude.

_____

_____

_____

_____

_____

_____

_____

_____

_____

_____

_____

_____

_____

_____

Be grateful.
Live in gratitude.
Live in appreciation.
Be appreciated.
Love.
And be loved.

_____

_____

_____

_____

_____

_____

_____

_____

_____

_____

_____

_____

_____

_____

_____

_____

_____

Support others
In receiving their gifts,
And your gifts
Will be received.

_____

_____

_____

_____

_____

_____

_____

_____

_____

_____

_____

_____

_____

_____

_____

_____

_____

Emotions run high
And low.
Just always
Let God know.

_____

_____

_____

_____

Moments are made
For memories to stay
In your heart
Each and every day.

_____

_____

_____

_____

_____

_____

_____

_____

_____

_____

_____

_____

_____

_____

_____

_____

Challenges are opportunities
In disguise.
Open your heart
And your eyes.

_____

_____

_____

_____

_____

_____

_____

_____

_____

_____

_____

_____

_____

_____

_____

_____

Life is a gift
Certainly not to miss
The creativity in you
Making all of your
Your dreams to come true.

_____

_____

_____

_____

_____

_____

_____

_____

_____

_____

_____

_____

_____

_____

_____

_____

Every day is a new perspective
In life
Guiding you to know
What is right.

_____

_____

_____

_____

Practice silence
In your mind.
Be ready for your dreams
To unwind.

_____

_____

_____

_____

_____

_____

_____

_____

_____

_____

_____

_____

_____

_____

_____

_____

You're a leader
In your own mind.
Now go ahead
And step up
To your potential.

_____

_____

_____

_____

_____

_____

_____

_____

_____

_____

_____

_____

_____

_____

_____

_____

_____

_____

_____

What life was
Could not be
Because life revolves
Around everything you see.

_____

_____

_____

_____

_____

_____

_____

_____

_____

_____

_____

_____

_____

_____

_____

_____

Life: Have to or Get to

You don't have to
You get to
Isn't it nice to know
That you're in control

To lead your life with Grace
And know you will be embraced

You see God wants you to know
You don't have to
You get to

Live your life in bliss
With pure happiness
Give your heart away
Each and everyday

But Remember
You don't have to
You get too

Your soul knows
How life goes.
Go with the flow
And let go.

_____

_____

_____

_____

_____

_____

_____

_____

_____

_____

_____

_____

_____

_____

_____

_____

_____

Be blessed
With who God created you to be . . .
Special,
Unique,
And made to believe.

_____

_____

_____

_____

_____

_____

_____

_____

_____

_____

_____

_____

_____

_____

_____

_____

_____

In life
Trying is a maybe;
Doing your best
Is a yes.

_____

_____

_____

_____

_____

_____

_____

_____

_____

_____

_____

_____

_____

_____

_____

_____

_____

_____

_____

Wake up and say
"I can"
And you will.

_____

_____

_____

_____

Live in endless possibilities
As you create the possible.

_____

_____

_____

_____

Letting go
Of what doesn't belong to you
Gives back energy
On what it is
You want to do.

_____

_____

_____

_____

_____

_____

_____

_____

_____

_____

_____

_____

_____

_____

_____

_____

_____

To have
And know true love
Is a gift
From God up above.

_____

_____

_____

_____

_____

_____

_____

_____

_____

_____

_____

_____

_____

_____

_____

_____

_____

With emotions running through your heart,
God is sending
Messages of inspiration
To share with you
For your day to start.

_____

_____

_____

_____

_____

_____

_____

_____

_____

_____

_____

_____

_____

_____

_____

_____

_____

Your gifts get stronger every day.
All you have to do
Is open your heart
And allow them to stay.

_____
_____
_____
_____
_____
_____
_____
_____
_____
_____
_____
_____
_____
_____
_____
_____
_____
_____
_____

Open your heart
And let the light in;
That's where love begins.

_____

_____

_____

_____

Walking in the light
Of fulfillment
Is living through God
In stillness.

_____

_____

_____

_____

_____

_____

_____

_____

_____

_____

_____

_____

_____

_____

_____

Positive energy
Is the light
That brings hope
Into your life.

_____

_____

_____

_____

_____

_____

_____

_____

_____

_____

_____

_____

_____

_____

_____

_____

Life is about caring and sharing.
When you do your part,
That's when you'll know
The real you
In everything you do.

_____

_____

_____

_____

_____

_____

_____

_____

_____

_____

_____

_____

_____

_____

_____

_____

Courageous you say to be brave;
Living in faith
Is the only way.

_____

_____

_____

_____

_____

_____

_____

_____

_____

_____

_____

_____

_____

_____

_____

_____

_____

Have you taken time
To live out your gifts?
Focus and clarity
Will let you live it.

_____

_____

_____

_____

_____

_____

_____

_____

_____

_____

_____

_____

_____

_____

_____

_____

_____

_____

Shedding a tear
Lets you know
Your heart is open
And someone is
Thinking of you up there.

_____

_____

_____

_____

_____

_____

_____

_____

_____

_____

_____

_____

_____

_____

_____

_____

Live the real you,
Not what someone else
Sees in you.

_____

_____

_____

_____

_____

_____

_____

_____

_____

_____

_____

_____

_____

_____

_____

_____

Surround yourself
Around happy people,
And you'll be
A happy person.

_____

_____

_____

_____

An awakening of our soul
Will give you
Many answers you hold.
Wake up your soul.

Be You

Are you running around looking for your life
And chasing for that advice
Did you know it was deep in your soul
For you to know

When you sit and relax and meditate
You will find that open gate
It has a golden key
Waiting for you to see
How amazing you can be

Now go ahead and unlock the gate
So that you can escape
From the things that you really don't want to do
So that you can be the real You

It's the little things
That count.
It's as simple as
A smile,
A hug,
And a prayer.

_____

_____

_____

_____

Your inner strength
Will never let you down.
It's always there
Every time you turn around.

_____

_____

_____

_____

Do
What you say you'll do.
Be the creator in you
In all you do.

_____

_____

_____

_____

Inspire with love
And in faith
In all you do.
There are many angels watching over you.

_____

_____

_____

_____

Be crystal clear
For your dreams to appear
Out of thin air.

_____

_____

_____

_____

_____

_____

_____

_____

_____

_____

_____

_____

_____

_____

_____

_____

We are here to change,
Not to be the same.
What do you want to change?

_____

_____

_____

_____

_____

_____

_____

_____

_____

_____

_____

_____

_____

_____

_____

_____

The light of life begins with you.
Living from the inside out
Will shine the light
On everyone around you.

_____

_____

_____

_____

_____

_____

_____

_____

_____

_____

_____

_____

_____

_____

_____

_____

Choices are given
To you every day,
With decisions to be made
Especially when you pray.

_____

_____

_____

_____

Judgment lives from within.
When you judge someone else,
You're judging yourself.

_____

_____

_____

_____

_____

_____

_____

_____

_____

_____

_____

_____

_____

_____

_____

_____

_____

You have to get comfortable
With being
Uncomfortable
To grow.

_____

_____

_____

_____

Face it . . .
Your every day is a reality
With God guiding you
To eternity.

_____

_____

_____

_____

_____

_____

_____

_____

_____

_____

_____

_____

_____

_____

_____

_____

_____

Who am I?
A gift from God
To serve and to love.

_____

_____

_____

_____

_____

_____

_____

_____

_____

_____

_____

_____

_____

_____

_____

_____

Time will not be
On your side;
It will allow you
To get by.

_____
_____
_____
_____

_____
_____
_____
_____
_____
_____
_____
_____
_____
_____
_____
_____
_____

Say "I love you"
Often.

_____

_____

_____

_____

_____

_____

_____

_____

_____

_____

_____

_____

_____

_____

_____

_____

_____

Appreciate life
With gratitude
Every day and night.

_____

_____

_____

_____

_____

_____

_____

_____

_____

_____

_____

_____

_____

_____

_____

_____

_____

Feel the brisk air
With mountains everywhere.
Relax your mind;
Let it unwind.

_____

_____

_____

_____

_____

_____

_____

_____

_____

_____

_____

_____

_____

_____

_____

_____

Guidance is a key
From your friends
And family.

_____

_____

_____

_____

_____

_____

_____

_____

_____

_____

_____

_____

_____

_____

_____

_____

_____

Believing in God's grace
Will open your heart
To be embraced.

_____

_____

_____

_____

Your present
Is living in the present.

_____

_____

_____

_____

_____

_____

_____

_____

_____

_____

_____

_____

_____

_____

_____

_____

_____

Shhh . . .
Speak less, Listen more

To grow and learn we must listen
Because that's what life is missing'

Open your ears and quiet your voice
Now you can begin to rejoice

Now that you have the rules down
Let's turn your life around

There's so much out there for you to see and to be
All you have to do is follow your heart and you will see

Remember to pray each and every day
Your dreams are waiting for you to play

Speak less and listen more
Life is great when you can explore

In the midst of the fog
You cannot see it all.
It's when you get through,
Your life opens up for you.

_____

_____

_____

_____

_____

_____

_____

_____

_____

_____

_____

_____

_____

_____

_____

_____

Live and let go
And open up your soul.

_____

_____

_____

_____

When you teach, not judge,
It will give you
More than you can
Think of.

_____

_____

_____

_____

Happiness is something
You don't have to buy;
All you have to do
Is allow it to stop by.

_____

_____

_____

_____

_____

_____

_____

_____

_____

_____

_____

_____

_____

_____

_____

_____

May faith lead you the way
Each and every day.

_____

_____

_____

_____

_____

_____

_____

_____

_____

_____

_____

_____

_____

_____

_____

_____

_____

To be valued
You must value
Everyone around you.

_____

_____

_____

_____

_____

_____

_____

_____

_____

_____

_____

_____

_____

_____

_____

_____

_____

Failures are lessons
To give you
The right perspective in life.

_____

_____

_____

_____

_____

_____

_____

_____

_____

_____

_____

_____

_____

_____

_____

_____

_____

Surround yourself
With the best
And you will feel
Your best.

_____

_____

_____

_____

_____

_____

_____

_____

_____

_____

_____

_____

_____

_____

_____

_____

_____

Know the "what" in your life,
Not the "how."
Send a message
To God to allow.

_____

_____

_____

_____

_____

_____

_____

_____

_____

_____

_____

_____

_____

_____

_____

_____

_____

_____

Love to serve
And serve to love.

_____

_____

_____

_____

_____

_____

_____

_____

_____

_____

_____

_____

_____

_____

_____

_____

_____

_____

Every day is new
Creating memories
Just for you.

_____

_____

_____

_____

Be brave;
Ride the wave.
Life is a journey.

_____

_____

_____

_____

Happiness is living
With God in your soul
In every moment
As you let go.

_____

_____

_____

_____

_____

_____

_____

_____

_____

_____

_____

_____

_____

_____

_____

_____

_____

Fulfilling your dreams
Is up to you.
Now go ahead
And let them come true.

_____

_____

_____

_____

_____

_____

_____

_____

_____

_____

_____

_____

_____

_____

_____

_____

_____

Living in the past
Will hold you back.
Living in the future
Is moving too fast.
But staying in the present moment
Is where life is at.

_____

_____

_____

_____

The power of acceptance
Is between you and God . . .
Your creating and believing
That it will come true,

_____

_____

_____

_____

_____

_____

_____

_____

_____

_____

_____

_____

_____

_____

_____

_____

_____

Life is a mystery . . .
Have faith
As you create your history.

_____

_____

_____

_____

We never know one's
Last day.
Why wait to share
Your love today.

_____

_____

_____

_____

_____

_____

_____

_____

_____

_____

_____

_____

_____

_____

_____

_____

_____

See your life through
A crystal ball,
A vision that
Lets you have it all.

_____

_____

_____

_____

_____

_____

_____

_____

_____

_____

_____

_____

_____

_____

_____

_____

_____

Angels are tapping on shoulders

When the Angels are tapping on your shoulders
It's because you're needed to be by someone's side
Every moment for them to get by

Now it's up to you
To follow through
With having so much to do
The Angels need you

When someone is heavy on your heart
Show them how much you care to be apart

You were put in God's plan
To give them a hand
To comfort and let them understand

That they are never alone as each day goes by
So let them know that you are by their side
Because you never know when they need to cry

We want to thank you in advance
For giving their life a chance

And showing your Love
With all of the Angels up above

So just know when you're getting that 'tap on your shoulders'
That you were chosen by Angels to guide them along
To make them feel strong

Know that you are assigned
With someone in mind
It is good to know the Angels have you
As the Angel send their love that is every so true

Life can change
Without your permission
And rearrange
Your mission.

_____

_____

_____

_____

_____

_____

_____

_____

_____

_____

_____

_____

_____

_____

_____

Life is not what we
Understand about someone else;
It's about what
We understand about oneself.

_____

_____

_____

_____

_____

_____

_____

_____

_____

_____

_____

_____

_____

_____

_____

_____

Life is simpler than you can imagine;
Living in gratitude and appreciation
Allows you to be grateful and appreciated.

_____

_____

_____

_____

Knowing that you can have
What you want
With a positive attitude
Allows you to have a lot.

_____

_____

_____

_____

Open your heart;
You'll be blessed.
It's your everyday gift
Not to miss.

_____

_____

_____

_____

_____

_____

_____

_____

_____

_____

_____

_____

_____

_____

_____

_____

Make up your mind.
Create your reality;
Watch it show up
With simplicity
Of your imagination.

_____

_____

_____

_____

_____

_____

_____

_____

_____

_____

_____

_____

_____

_____

_____

_____

_____

Life is about happiness.
Your inner soul
Knows what life holds.

_____

_____

_____

_____

_____

_____

_____

_____

_____

_____

_____

_____

_____

_____

_____

Communication is the key.
There's so much out there
For you to receive.
All you have to do
Is believe.

_____

_____

_____

_____

_____

_____

_____

_____

_____

_____

_____

_____

_____

_____

_____

Life is a journey . . .
As you walk your path,
The outcome is revealed
Each moment of your dash.

_____

_____

_____

_____

_____

_____

_____

_____

_____

_____

_____

_____

_____

_____

_____

_____

_____

_____

God will always
Lead you to your path
As long as
You leave the door open.

_____

_____

_____

_____

_____

_____

_____

_____

_____

_____

_____

_____

_____

_____

_____

_____

Time is not
Given back.
Capture your moments
So they will last.

_____

_____

_____

_____

_____

_____

_____

_____

_____

_____

_____

_____

_____

_____

_____

_____

_____

Allowing someone
To steal your thunder
Puts you in the rain
And them in your sunshine.

_____

_____

_____

_____

God changes our lives for a reason.
It's about accepting
To where you have been
To where you are going.

_____

_____

_____

_____

_____

_____

_____

_____

_____

_____

_____

_____

_____

_____

_____

_____

_____

_____

As we bloom
Each and every day,
Our hearts will
Open up as we pray.

_____

_____

_____

_____

_____

_____

_____

_____

_____

_____

_____

_____

_____

_____

_____

_____

_____

Getting uncomfortable to grow
Will be an open door
You didn't know.

_____

_____

_____

_____

_____

_____

_____

_____

_____

_____

_____

_____

_____

_____

_____

_____

_____

When your life
Is put to a test,
It's to let you see
Your strength at its best.

_____

_____

_____

_____

_____

_____

_____

_____

_____

_____

_____

_____

_____

_____

_____

_____

Once you realize
You don't own anything
And know that everything
Is on loan from God,
Your life will become
Much more flexible.

_____

_____

_____

_____

_____

_____

_____

_____

_____

_____

_____

_____

_____

_____

A balanced life
Is a happy life.
Take care of you
In everything you do.

_____

_____

_____

_____

_____

_____

_____

_____

_____

_____

_____

_____

_____

_____

_____

_____

Motivation from within
Is how you will win
To live your journey
By living your purpose
With passion.

_____

_____

_____

_____

_____

_____

_____

_____

_____

_____

_____

_____

_____

_____

_____

_____

_____

It's The Simple Things

It's the simple things in life that count
Without a doubt
When you share your heart
You'll feel that spark

We are given blessings everyday
Just know it starts when we pray
When you put a smile on someone's face
Know that it cannot be replaced

It's the simple things in life that count
With every moment from here on out
When you have something to share
Know that person really cares

As I share this message with you
Open your heart with someone new
It's because you are someone special too
And there is someone out there waiting for you

To make a difference in their life
Because it's the simple things
In life that count
Without a doubt

Live in gratitude with love.
Appreciate everything around you.
Miracles will happen
With many blessings.

_____

_____

_____

_____

_____

_____

_____

_____

_____

_____

_____

_____

_____

_____

_____

_____

_____

Life is a climb . . .
Waiting for you to find
The inner you
With many blessings too.

_____

_____

_____

_____

Blessings come every day.
It's living in appreciation
Is how they stay.

_____

_____

_____

_____

_____

_____

_____

_____

_____

_____

_____

_____

_____

_____

_____

_____

_____

_____

What you focus on
You'll receive.
Now go ahead
And focus on
What you believe.

_____

_____

_____

_____

As you view life,
God is there holding you tight
Watching you in all you do
And creating miracles too.

_____

_____

_____

_____

_____

_____

_____

_____

_____

_____

_____

_____

_____

_____

_____

_____

Life changes
Every moment of the day.
It's knowing
That God is with you
Each and every time you pray.

_____

_____

_____

_____

_____

_____

_____

_____

_____

_____

_____

_____

_____

_____

_____

_____

_____

We're here to learn
About ourselves
And to bring joy and happiness
To everyone else.

_____

_____

_____

_____

Every moment in time
Is a once-in-a-lifetime.
Expand your mind
And open your heart.
Always keep God a part.

_____

_____

_____

_____

Always strive to be
And to do your best,
God will take care of the rest.

_____

_____

_____

_____

_____

_____

_____

_____

_____

_____

_____

_____

_____

_____

_____

_____

_____

_____

You can change
Someone's life
With one word . . .
Love.

_____

_____

_____

_____

_____

_____

_____

_____

_____

_____

_____

_____

_____

_____

_____

_____

_____

There are many blessings
That are ignited in
The power of prayer.
Taking the time
Will allow them to align.

_____

_____

_____

_____

_____

_____

_____

_____

_____

_____

_____

_____

_____

_____

_____

_____

Life is about being happy
And to know who you really are.
As you open your heart,
You'll find it's not that far.

_____

_____

_____

_____

_____

_____

_____

_____

_____

_____

_____

_____

_____

_____

_____

_____

When your soul
Wakes up,
You'll know more
Than you ever
Thought you knew.

_____

_____

_____

_____

_____

_____

_____

_____

_____

_____

_____

_____

_____

_____

_____

_____

Life unfolds
Every moment of the day.
Paying attention
To what matters most
Allows it to stay.

_____

_____

_____

_____

_____

_____

_____

_____

_____

_____

_____

_____

_____

_____

_____

As we realize what matters most
Is when we will share what is close
To our hearts today
And every day.

_____

_____

_____

_____

Create an abundance of love
In your life.
You'll see miracles
Show up every day and night.

_____

_____

_____

_____

_____
_____
_____
_____
_____
_____
_____
_____
_____
_____
_____
_____
_____

Clarity is key
While living your
Purpose and passion.
Let the light in
As your new day begins.

_____

_____

_____

_____

Listening to your heart
Will start
Your new beginning of your day
As you create and
Share your love today.

_____

_____

_____

_____

_____

_____

_____

_____

_____

_____

_____

_____

_____

_____

_____

_____

_____

_____

Your journey
Is to discover you.
Open your heart;
You will find
Your blessings are within you.

_____

_____

_____

_____

_____

_____

_____

_____

_____

_____

_____

_____

_____

_____

_____

_____

_____

_____

Too Busy

When life gets too Busy and steps in the way
At time you won't know what to do or say
You might have to step back because your life can slip away

There are so many things you must do and get done
What you must know is that you don't have to run

Life shares an experience you must understand
Slow down your Busy so you can live in God's plan

Enjoy yourself while your here
And always show how much you care
You must know there's not much time to spare
So remember to spread your love everywhere

Now take a deep breathe and slow down you see
How much of life you are taken from me
To make this simple as can be
Go ahead and close your eyes and relax with me

Love is why you're here;
Go ahead and share.
Your heart holds the key
For everyone to see.

_____

_____

_____

_____

_____

_____

_____

_____

_____

_____

_____

_____

_____

_____

_____

_____

_____

_____

Hold on to your dreams
With faith and love.
Know that God is taking care of you
From up above.

_____

_____

_____

_____

_____

_____

_____

_____

_____

_____

_____

_____

_____

_____

_____

_____

Awareness is living
In the present moment,
Focusing on your intention
With attention.

_____

_____

_____

_____

_____

_____

_____

_____

_____

_____

_____

_____

_____

_____

_____

_____

_____

Own your power;
Know who you are.
Now, go ahead and
Reach for the stars.

_____

_____

_____

_____

_____

_____

_____

_____

_____

_____

_____

_____

_____

_____

_____

On the outside, we are so strong.
Then there are times
We pray
To get along.

_____

_____

_____

_____

_____

_____

_____

_____

_____

_____

_____

_____

_____

_____

_____

_____

Recognize who is
In your life today.
You will never know
How long they will stay.

———————————————

———————————————

———————————————

———————————————

———————————————
———————————————
———————————————
———————————————
———————————————
———————————————
———————————————
———————————————
———————————————
———————————————
———————————————
———————————————
———————————————

A balanced life
Is a happy life.
Take care of you
In everything you do.

_____

_____

_____

_____

Persistence,
Patience, and
Perseverance
Prevails your
Purpose.

_____

_____

_____

_____

_____

_____

_____

_____

_____

_____

_____

_____

_____

_____

_____

_____

_____

_____

Having God
Close to your heart
Is a great way
For your day to start.

_____

_____

_____

_____

_____

_____

_____

_____

_____

_____

_____

_____

_____

_____

_____

_____

_____

When you get out
Of your own way,
Miracles will happen
Every day.

_____

_____

_____

_____

_____

_____

_____

_____

_____

_____

_____

_____

_____

_____

_____

_____

_____

_____

You don't have to imagine
Your life
In someone else's shoes;
Your life was designed just for you.

_____

_____

_____

_____

_____

_____

_____

_____

_____

_____

_____

_____

_____

_____

_____

_____

_____

Life has much to gain;
Yet there will be
Some pain.
Let faith in
To let your life
Live from within.

_____

_____

_____

_____

_____
_____
_____
_____
_____
_____
_____
_____
_____
_____
_____
_____
_____

Creating each moment
Starts with you.
What is it
You want to do?
Know your "what"
For it to show up.

_____

_____

_____

_____

_____

_____

_____

_____

_____

_____

_____

_____

_____

_____

_____

Forgiveness
Expands the real you
To become and be
What you came to do.

_____

_____

_____

_____

_____

_____

_____

_____

_____

_____

_____

_____

_____

_____

_____

Taking time in life
To breathe
Is what we all need.

_____

_____

_____

_____

_____

_____

_____

_____

_____

_____

_____

_____

_____

_____

_____

_____

Believing in your dream
Creates the energy
To see the light
And to bring it to life.

_____

_____

_____

_____

_____

_____

_____

_____

_____

_____

_____

_____

_____

_____

_____

_____

Love will win
Every time.
Open your heart
And your mind.

_____

_____

_____

_____

_____

_____

_____

_____

_____

_____

_____

_____

_____

_____

_____

_____

_____

Sunsets are a gift to you
To count your blessings
And your next day too.

_____

_____

_____

_____

_____

_____

_____

_____

_____

_____

_____

_____

_____

_____

_____

_____

_____

Your journey
Is for you to see
How much
You believe.

_____

_____

_____

_____

_____

_____

_____

_____

_____

_____

_____

_____

_____

_____

_____

_____

Faith and Trust

As your soul touches you deep inside
There is one thing that you'll have to do to let you get by
Believe
In you
Will do

It will get us there
No matter where we are
We're not really that far

Having Faith and Trust
Is a must

We will be guided by a light
As we see what is in sight

What has been waiting for us to know
Is in our soul

Which holds the key
For our reality
Are you ready to see
What you can be

Faith and Trust
In you
Will do

The unknown
Is the healing
To the known.

_____

_____

_____

_____

_____

_____

_____

_____

_____

_____

_____

_____

_____

_____

_____

_____

_____

Messengers
Are who we came to be
To share with the world
Reality.

_____

_____

_____

_____

_____

_____

_____

_____

_____

_____

_____

_____

_____

_____

_____

_____

_____

_____

May your life
Be the difference
You've been waiting for.

_____

_____

_____

_____

_____

_____

_____

_____

_____

_____

_____

_____

_____

_____

_____

_____

Your journey
To happiness
Will inspire you
Along the way
As you believe it will stay.

_____

_____

_____

_____

_____

_____

_____

_____

_____

_____

_____

_____

_____

_____

_____

_____

You deserve
The best.
Why not
Expect the best?

_____

_____

_____

_____

Dreams are put on hold
To give you
Strength and courage
As they unfold.

_____

_____

_____

_____

_____

_____

_____

_____

_____

_____

_____

_____

_____

_____

_____

Pain fuels your soul
To give you courage and strength
To live and let go.

_____

_____

_____

_____

_____

_____

_____

_____

_____

_____

_____

_____

_____

_____

_____

_____

_____

_____

As you are open
To receive messages
From God,
Be ready to change.

_____

_____

_____

_____

_____

_____

_____

_____

_____

_____

_____

_____

_____

_____

_____

_____

_____

Confirmation in life
Will show up
When it's just right.

_____

_____

_____

_____

_____

_____

_____

_____

_____

_____

_____

_____

_____

_____

_____

_____

Life unfolds right in front of you.
Are you creating
Everything
That you wanted to do?

_____

_____

_____

_____

_____

_____

_____

_____

_____

_____

_____

_____

_____

_____

As life floats by,
Fulfill your dreams
And your "why."

_____

_____

_____

_____

_____

_____

_____

_____

_____

_____

_____

_____

_____

_____

_____

_____

_____

_____

Stepping out of your
Comfort zone
May not be easy.
It's all about your
Faith and believing.

_____

_____

_____

_____

A prayer room is a sacred place
Where you get to release
And feel embraced.
Knowing that God is in control
Allows you to live and let go.

_____

_____

_____

_____

_____

_____

_____

_____

_____

_____

_____

_____

_____

_____

_____

_____

Listening to your intuition
Will always guide you
To your mission.

_____

_____

_____

_____

_____

_____

_____

_____

_____

_____

_____

_____

_____

_____

_____

_____

_____

_____

Live in gratitude with love.
Appreciate everything around you
And miracles will happen
With many blessings.

_____

_____

_____

_____

_____

_____

_____

_____

_____

_____

_____

_____

_____

_____

_____

_____

Combining faith and love
Lets you know
What you are made of.

_____

_____

_____

_____

_____

_____

_____

_____

_____

_____

_____

_____

_____

_____

_____

God knows what He is doing.
You have to take a
Leap of faith
To your destiny.

_____

_____

_____

_____

_____

_____

_____

_____

_____

_____

_____

_____

_____

_____

_____

_____

Life is a puzzle
With many pieces,
A collection of you
Wanting you to believe
In what it is you want to do.

_____

_____

_____

_____

_____

_____

_____

_____

_____

_____

_____

_____

_____

_____

_____

_____

At times
Life is a thought process,
Thinking about
Where you are
And where you are going to go.

_____

_____

_____

_____

Your Dream

Life is a journey right from the start
Some just wonder where it starts

It's not something you can see or read
It's way deep inside you see

It's nothing that anyone can tell you to be
Just open your heart and soul
And listen to your guidance which you do hold

Take a moment each night and day
As you begin to pray

Quiet your mind and allow yourself to breathe
You will see what your dream has been wanting to be

You have covered it up with so much sound
That's why it couldn't be found

The square of life--
Faith ~ Love ~ Commitment ~ Communication--
It's the golden key
Of the way life is to be.

_____

_____

_____

_____

Life is a process . . .
It's all about you
To discover new.

_____

_____

_____

_____

_____

_____

_____

_____

_____

_____

_____

_____

_____

_____

_____

_____

Love is kind and beautiful
Right from the start,
And it comes from your heart .
Love can take your breath away
Simply every day.

_____

_____

_____

_____

_____

_____

_____

_____

_____

_____

_____

_____

_____

_____

_____

Opening your heart to faith
Allows you to live your life
In amazing grace.

_____

_____

_____

_____

Seasons are the start
Of a new beginning
Letting your heart know
To live and let go.

_____

_____

_____

_____

_____

_____

_____

_____

_____

_____

_____

_____

_____

_____

_____

_____

_____

_____

You're a mirror of you.
As you are grateful to others,
You will live in gratitude.

_____

_____

_____

_____

_____

_____

_____

_____

_____

_____

_____

_____

_____

_____

_____

_____

_____

What is a dragonfly to be?
A cross with angel wings
Letting you know to fly
Because faith
Is always on your side.

_____

_____

_____

_____

_____

_____

_____

_____

_____

_____

_____

_____

_____

_____

_____

The key is within you
For your doors to open.
As you unlock them,
You'll see everything
You came to be.

_____

_____

_____

_____

_____

_____

_____

_____

_____

_____

_____

_____

_____

_____

_____

_____

_____

_____

When your life is put to a test,
It's to let you see
Your strength at its best.
Now go ahead and stay strong;
Staying in faith is where you belong.

_____

_____

_____

_____

_____

_____

_____

_____

_____

_____

_____

_____

_____

_____

_____

_____

_____

_____

Your strength is in others.
Paying attention to what
They bring to you
Is what makes you stronger.

_____

_____

_____

_____

_____

_____

_____

_____

_____

_____

_____

_____

_____

_____

_____

Let go of what is
Holding you back
By confirming what is yours
If you really want it.

_____

_____

_____

_____

_____

_____

_____

_____

_____

_____

_____

_____

_____

_____

_____

_____

Timing is everything.
Once it aligns with you,
It will show up
Without your expecting it.
Now that's a miracle within itself.

_____

_____

_____

_____

_____

_____

_____

_____

_____

_____

_____

_____

_____

_____

_____

_____

Love how each and every day
Has been already planned for you,
And know all you have to do
Is walk through it.

Everyone walks in their own shoes.
There's no way anyone would know
Or understand another human's soul.

_____

_____

_____

_____

_____

_____

_____

_____

_____

_____

_____

_____

_____

_____

_____

_____

_____

_____

Recognizing the change
That someone has made in your life
Will make the difference in you
In everything you do

_____

_____

_____

_____

As time passes by,
Don't forget your "why."

_____

_____

_____

_____

_____

_____

_____

_____

_____

_____

_____

_____

_____

_____

_____

_____

_____

_____

Finding ourselves
Is a learning process.
Live in faith and trust,
And know that God is a must.

_____

_____

_____

_____

Once a day goes by
It's gone forever.
Embrace your every moment
In gratitude with love.

_____

_____

_____

_____

_____

_____

_____

_____

_____

_____

_____

_____

_____

_____

_____

_____

_____

Create an abundance of love
In your life.
You will see miracles
Show up every day and night.

_____

_____

_____

_____

_____

_____

_____

_____

_____

_____

_____

_____

_____

_____

_____

_____

_____

Human Being or Human Doing

What are you being in life
Someone who lives to do what's right
Or someone who's doing, not seeing what's in sight

Are you experiencing a new day
Or living your life the same way

Are you taking life in one big gulp
Or enjoying it one bite at a time

Is your doing moving to fast
Or are you being to make life last

Is your being valuing your time
Or is your doing making you busy all the time

Now that you see what life can be
Enjoy your being, let go of your doing
Having time for you
Is important to do

Clarity is key
While living your
Purpose with passion.
Let the light in
As your new day begins.

_____

_____

_____

_____

_____

_____

_____

_____

_____

_____

_____

_____

_____

_____

_____

_____

_____

_____

Listening to your heart
Will start the new
Beginning of your day
As you create
And share your love today.

_____

_____

_____

_____

_____

_____

_____

_____

_____

_____

_____

_____

_____

_____

It takes one person to change
Your life.
Be patient; he or she will show up
When the time is right.

_____

_____

_____

_____

_____

_____

_____

_____

_____

_____

_____

_____

_____

_____

_____

_____

_____

Failures are blessings
To your destination
Guiding you on your journey.

_____

_____

_____

_____

_____

_____

_____

_____

_____

_____

_____

_____

_____

_____

_____

_____

_____

_____

Whatever is lost
Will be found
Because our soul
Will never let you down.

_____

_____

_____

_____

_____

_____

_____

_____

_____

_____

_____

_____

_____

_____

_____

Fulfilling your dreams
Is up to you.
Now go ahead
And let them come true.

_____

_____

_____

_____

The gift of wisdom
Is the greatest gift
Of all.

_____

_____

_____

_____

_____

_____

_____

_____

_____

_____

_____

_____

_____

_____

_____

_____

_____

Every moment is a new memory.
Allow the process to grow
And belong to you.
You are very special
And have a gift to share.

_____

_____

_____

_____

_____

_____

_____

_____

_____

_____

_____

_____

_____

_____

_____

_____

To be genuine
Is to tap in to
Your higher self
And to care
For everyone else.

_____

_____

_____

_____

_____

_____

_____

_____

_____

_____

_____

_____

_____

_____

_____

_____

What "is"
And what life "should be"
Is for
Your future to see.

_____

_____

_____

_____

_____

_____

_____

_____

_____

_____

_____

_____

_____

_____

_____

_____

_____

There will be clues in your life
To show you
Your passion in sight.
Follow the breadcrumbs;
It's your map to ignite
Your purpose to let you know it's right.

_____

_____

_____

_____

_____

_____

_____

_____

_____

_____

_____

_____

_____

_____

_____

_____

_____

With every step you take,
Realize time is precious.
Create every moment
To be timeless.

_____

_____

_____

_____

_____

_____

_____

_____

_____

_____

_____

_____

_____

_____

_____

_____

Everything in life
Is in the asking.
Create what you want to do;
Now watch it come true.

_____

_____

_____

_____

It's the quality of time
You spend on this earth;
Value it and understand
What it is worth.

_____

_____

_____

_____

_____

_____

_____

_____

_____

_____

_____

_____

_____

_____

_____

_____

_____

_____

Showing who you love
Is such an important part of who you are.
It's the memories that you make
That will lead you to God's grace.

_____

_____

_____

_____

_____

_____

_____

_____

_____

_____

_____

_____

_____

_____

_____

_____

Uncertainty is a perception
Of life.
Go with the flow
And know you'll be all right.

_____

_____

_____

_____

_____

_____

_____

_____

_____

_____

_____

_____

_____

_____

Patience is love
And gives you time
To treasure each moment

_____

_____

_____

_____

Predicting your tomorrow
Takes away your feelings from today

_____

_____

_____

_____

_____

_____

_____

_____

_____

_____

_____

_____

_____

_____

_____

_____

_____

_____

Love is so kind and beautiful.
You must find it from within
Because yes,
That's where it begins.

_____

_____

_____

_____

_____

_____

_____

_____

_____

_____

_____

_____

_____

_____

_____

_____

Life Choices

You have life choices to control everyday
There is a price to pay
That may not be displayed

Choices are a gift to you in the now
Go ahead and choose wisely and allow

When you heart speaks loud and clear
All you have to do is hear

Your choices are made way deep inside
All you have to do is abide

It's really so magical as when it's a yes
Your body will tingle without a guess

As for when it's a no and doesn't seem right
You'll have a pause to make you think twice

So just remember the choices can be bliss
Or just a near miss

Enjoy your life choices today
All you have to do is pray

Love is like a rainbow
From beginning to end.
Love can skip a beat
Until you feel complete.

_____

_____

_____

_____

_____

_____

_____

_____

_____

_____

_____

_____

_____

_____

_____

_____

_____

_____

_____

_____

Giving up on an
Opportunity to listen
Is giving up on an
Opportunity to share
Your love.

_____

_____

_____

_____

_____

_____

_____

_____

_____

_____

_____

_____

_____

_____

_____

If you don't ask,
It's a "no."
If you do ask,
It's a "possibility."

_____

_____

_____

_____

_____

_____

_____

_____

_____

_____

_____

_____

_____

_____

_____

When the angels are tapping on your shoulders,
It's because you are needed
To be by someone's side
Every moment for them to get by.

_____

_____

_____

_____

_____

_____

_____

_____

_____

_____

_____

_____

_____

_____

_____

_____

_____

_____

_____

You were put in God's plan
To give a hand,
To comfort,
And to let others understand.

_____

_____

_____

_____

Courageous
You are made to be.
Yes, we hold the key
For our own reality.

_____

_____

_____

_____

_____

_____

_____

_____

_____

_____

_____

_____

_____

_____

_____

Thanks for showing up
In my life.
You made things simple and right.

_____

_____

_____

_____

_____

_____

_____

_____

_____

_____

_____

_____

_____

_____

_____

_____

_____

You are such a gift from God
Who watches our every moment,
Knows what we need,
And brings it down
For all to see.

_____

_____

_____

_____

_____

_____

_____

_____

_____

_____

_____

_____

_____

_____

_____

_____

_____

A princess angel you are
As I reach for the stars
And hold you in my arms.

_____

_____

_____

_____

_____

_____

_____

_____

_____

_____

_____

_____

_____

_____

_____

_____

_____

When life gets too busy,
You cannot see.
Slow down your busy
And be set free.

_____

_____

_____

_____

_____

_____

_____

_____

_____

_____

_____

_____

_____

_____

_____

Your beauty lives from within,
Creating possibilities
To begin
The change that is within you,
Making a difference
In what you want to do.

_____

_____

_____

_____

_____

_____

_____

_____

_____

_____

_____

_____

_____

_____

_____

_____

Believe ~ Know
All you have to do is ask
To complete your many tasks.

_____

_____

_____

_____

_____

_____

_____

_____

_____

_____

_____

_____

_____

_____

_____

_____

Open your heart
To know your loveliness.
It's your journey
To create this fullness
In your
Mind ~ Body ~ Soul.

_____

_____

_____

_____

_____

_____

_____

_____

_____

_____

_____

_____

_____

_____

_____

_____

Be brave.
Have courage
With patience.

_____

_____

_____

_____

Open your heart to faith.
Believe in God's grace;
Live in fullness
Of trusting who you are.

_____

_____

_____

_____

_____

_____

_____

_____

_____

_____

_____

_____

_____

_____

_____

_____

Releasing as you let go
Miraculously allows you control
Of choices that life gives you.

_____

_____

_____

_____

_____

_____

_____

_____

_____

_____

_____

_____

_____

_____

_____

_____

We are all the same
But different,
Sharing our unique gifts
In a special way.

_____

_____

_____

_____

_____

_____

_____

_____

_____

_____

_____

_____

_____

_____

_____

_____

_____

One moment at a time
Is your great Divine.
All you have to do is
Trust in God.

_____

_____

_____

_____

_____

_____

_____

_____

_____

_____

_____

_____

_____

_____

_____

_____

_____

Reach out with
Grace and faith.
Life is a stream of hope
To ignite our souls,
To believe,
And to know who we are.

_____

_____

_____

_____

_____

_____

_____

_____

_____

_____

_____

_____

_____

_____

_____

_____

_____

Live Your Passion

Have you ever thought what your would miss
If you didn't allow your Passion to exist

Time will slip away
Like no other today
You will for sure lose
If you don't move
Is you Passion on snooze?

With ever step you take
There might be mistakes
You must know that you will be guided there
Until you are near

Then your Passion will exist
And you will know
Which path you have missed

So go ahead and live your Passion in bliss
Because that's your superior happiness

Now doesn't life seem so grand
When you understand
Your Passion was there waiting for you
To know the real You, was all you had to do

In spite of conditions and convenience
And choices,
We are here to receive grace
And put it into the world.

_____

_____

_____

_____

Caring with compassion and love
Is a commitment
To your soul
From above.

_____

_____

_____

_____

_____

_____

_____

_____

_____

_____

_____

_____

_____

_____

_____

_____

Many blessings are ignited through
The power of prayer.
Quieting your mind
Will let them unwind.

_____

_____

_____

_____

Listening to the whispers
Sent to your heart
Will guide you
Each moment to start.

_____

_____

_____

_____

_____

_____

_____

_____

_____

_____

_____

_____

_____

_____

_____

_____

Messages are the key,
And you will see
Your many gifts
Are waiting for you to
"Just believe."

_____

_____

_____

_____

_____

_____

_____

_____

_____

_____

_____

_____

_____

_____

_____

_____

Ignite the spark in your soul
By living in prayer.
Now let go . . .
Knowing God is in control.

_____

_____

_____

_____

_____

_____

_____

_____

_____

_____

_____

_____

_____

_____

_____

Being strong allows you to carry on,
Knowing in your heart
Faith will guide you.

_____

_____

_____

_____

_____

_____

_____

_____

_____

_____

_____

_____

_____

_____

_____

A
Positive attitude
Will give you
Much gratitude.

_____

_____

_____

_____

_____

_____

_____

_____

_____

_____

_____

_____

_____

_____

_____

_____

Remaining faithful
To God every moment
Will give you strength
You didn't know.

_____

_____

_____

_____

_____

_____

_____

_____

_____

_____

_____

_____

_____

_____

_____

God will give you only
What you can handle,
Knowing the real you
Is being you.

_____

_____

_____

_____

_____

_____

_____

_____

_____

_____

_____

_____

_____

_____

_____

Life is a mystery
With so much history.
Courage is the key
For you all to see.

_____

_____

_____

_____

_____

_____

_____

_____

_____

_____

_____

_____

_____

_____

_____

_____

We're all one
Creating our being,
Not always knowing
What we are seeing.

_____

_____

_____

_____

_____

_____

_____

_____

_____

_____

_____

_____

_____

_____

_____

Limitlessness . . .
Togetherness . . .
Brings life and love together
Forever and ever.

_____

_____

_____

_____

_____

_____

_____

_____

_____

_____

_____

_____

_____

_____

_____

_____

_____

Knowing everyone around us is
Unique and surreal,
With many blessings
That make us so real.

_____

_____

_____

_____

_____

_____

_____

_____

_____

_____

_____

_____

_____

_____

_____

Eternal life begins from within;
Trusting in yourself will do.
Our soul whispers
Many answers guiding us.

_____

_____

_____

_____

_____

_____

_____

_____

_____

_____

_____

_____

_____

_____

_____

_____

_____

Allow faith to open our hearts
Daily for us to start.
God knows all about us
And our next day too.

_____

_____

_____

_____

_____
_____
_____
_____
_____
_____
_____
_____
_____
_____
_____

Knowing how our inner strength
Becomes stronger
As we help others along
Supporting a mission to discover new
Brings out the real you.

_____

_____

_____

_____

_____

_____

_____

_____

_____

_____

_____

_____

_____

_____

_____

_____

_____

_____

Having a preference in life
Will give you more insight.

_____

_____

_____

_____

Speak it loud and clear
And it will be there.
Your wishes and dreams
Will come true.
You just have to know
What it is you want to do.

_____

_____

_____

_____

_____

_____

_____

_____

_____

_____

_____

_____

_____

_____

_____

_____

God is With You

Whichever way you want to say
Everyday your soul wants to play

You have a mission to get done
A dream you call it here on earth

God is choosing with you not for you
Yes. . . you hold the key to your reality

You're guided with every step you take
For your human sake

Close the gap to get close to God
You'll feel a sigh of fresh air
Letting you know that he is there

God loves you and keeps you close
Because he cares for you the most

You will find the true you that you came to be
Allow your heat to become free
Unlocked with your key to life's reality

Here's the key to believe
Seek for good
Seek for better
Seek for you
That's all you have to do

Now it's time you become one
Embrace that you chose
God to be with you

We are all different;
Let's make a difference!

_____

_____

_____

_____

_____

_____

_____

_____

_____

_____

_____

_____

_____

_____

_____

_____

You have a guidance system
That has no resistance.
Follow it with your soul
Because it's a precious goal.

_____

_____

_____

_____

_____

_____

_____

_____

_____

_____

_____

_____

_____

_____

_____

_____

_____

_____

Don't doubt yourself
You were born with a gift.
Know that all you have to do
Is live life in bliss.

_____

_____

_____

_____

_____

_____

_____

_____

_____

_____

_____

_____

_____

_____

_____

_____

_____

_____

A guiding light
Will guide you
Both day and night.
It can be the sun,
The moon, or a star,
No matter where you are.

_____

_____

_____

_____

_____

_____

_____

_____

_____

_____

_____

_____

_____

_____

_____

_____

Supporting each other
Is a way to start;
It will unlock your heart.

_____

_____

_____

_____

_____

_____

_____

_____

_____

_____

_____

_____

_____

_____

_____

_____

_____

_____

Make everyone feel important;
It is the best key to have.
It will open your heart
To allow you to live within
Again and again
To let you know where life begins.

_____

_____

_____

_____

Synchronicity is all around you,
Giving you signs on what to do.
Are you listening
With your heart and soul
To allow the answers
To be told?

_____

_____

_____

_____

_____

_____

_____

_____

_____

_____

_____

_____

_____

_____

_____

When you are still,
You will hear
What is planned
For you here.

_____

_____

_____

_____

_____

_____

_____

_____

_____

_____

_____

_____

_____

_____

_____

Let your purpose
On this earth
Begin with your passion
That was given at birth.

_____

_____

_____

_____

_____

_____

_____

_____

_____

_____

_____

_____

_____

_____

As you turn the page
To another day,
You will create memories
To stay.

_____

_____

_____

_____

_____

_____

_____

_____

_____

_____

_____

_____

_____

_____

_____

_____

There are many things in life
That don't require a price tag.
Faith .. Love . . . Hope . . .
Will allow you to live rich and happy.

_____

_____

_____

_____

_____

_____

_____

_____

_____

_____

_____

_____

_____

_____

_____

_____

_____

Giving and receiving . . .
The more you give away,
The more you will receive every day.

       _____

       _____

       _____

       _____

Life is about taking the time
To know who you are.
Slowing down your busy
Is when you will realize that.

_____

_____

_____

_____

_____

_____

_____

_____

_____

_____

_____

_____

_____

_____

_____

_____

_____

Know that God
Is not done with you;
He will guide you
With what to do.

_____

_____

_____

_____

_____

_____

_____

_____

_____

_____

_____

_____

_____

_____

_____

_____

_____

At times we will fall.
Getting back up again
Is what makes us stronger.

_____

_____

_____

_____

_____

_____

_____

_____

_____

_____

_____

_____

_____

_____

_____

_____

_____

_____

Go ahead and share a smile
And know it's worth every mile.

_____

_____

_____

_____

_____

_____

_____

_____

_____

_____

_____

_____

_____

_____

_____

_____

Go ahead and open your heart
And breathe within.
Then feel the calmness;
That's where it begins.

_____

_____

_____

_____

_____

_____

_____

_____

_____

_____

_____

_____

_____

_____

_____

_____

_____

Now you can see the stars
Twinkle through the night
Waiting for you
In the morning light.

_____

_____

_____

_____

_____

_____

_____

_____

_____

_____

_____

_____

_____

_____

_____

Carry on
With your wish
As you see
Today;
Turn it into reality.

_____

_____

_____

_____

_____

_____

_____

_____

_____

_____

_____

_____

_____

_____

_____

_____

_____

There's an open door
Waiting just for you
To see how you will do
Making your dreams come true.

_____

_____

_____

_____

Life is an invitation
For the world to see
How brilliant
You can be.

_____

_____

_____

_____

_____

_____

_____

_____

_____

_____

_____

_____

_____

_____

_____

_____

_____

Go ahead and live out
Your dreams tonight.
How it must feel
To know that it is in sight.

_____

_____

_____

_____

_____

_____

_____

_____

_____

_____

_____

_____

_____

_____

_____

_____

When you are in love
With your dreams tonight
And now see them in sight,
You will never want to let them go.

_____

_____

_____

_____

_____

_____

_____

_____

_____

_____

_____

_____

_____

_____

_____

_____

Good Bye meets Hello

I had you at Hello and Good Bye
And I want you to know that my heart wants to cry
As I wipe each tear drop away, I just want to say
I LOVE YOU
There is no pain like this
That I thought even exist
Especially when you are so missed

Please send the Angels down
To let me know that you're around
Every time I begin to pray
I send my Love to you everyday
I'm just waiting for when
I get to see you again…

And It's great to know
That our Good Bye will be another Hello

Acknowledgements

I am thankful for my family and friends who have been there for me throughout my new journey, a path I never thought to be on. I want to thank you all for sharing your caring heartfelt love for and to me. I wouldn't be who I am today without all of you! You all know who you are . . . I truly love and appreciate you all.

I had never written a poem until days after losing the love of my life of 42 years. God showed up in a way I never knew existed. My heart opened up like a fireworks display. Realizing that we are all on our own individual journey woke up my soul. I couldn't stop and didn't want to stop listening to the messages that were coming to me, I felt truly blessed to have such an inner connection with my soul.

A Conversation with My Soul will not only be inspiring to *YOUR* soul but will uplift you when needed most.

Appreciate who is in your life with love and know how special they are to show up, a gift from God. They're your gift to show you true happiness. Most of all realize how important they are to YOU!

About the Author

Dixie Daly, lives in Colorado, where she and her family call home. Dixie's an Entrepreneur, Inventor, Author and business-to-business connector. Dixie combines her entrepreneurial energy with a lifelong passion for helping others and generously shares her expertise and extensive network of contacts to encourage others.

Dixie an award-winning poet enables others to believe in themselves and make their dreams come true. "Your dream is waiting for you to show up!" she says, "All you have to do is ask!" People relate to the honest emotions and passion in her poetry. They get caught up in her enthusiasm; they feel inspired and ready to look at life in a different way.

Having the opportunity to dance in her locally-produced "Dancing with the Stars," allowed Dixie to win a part of her heart back. This experience was life altering, she said. "It took getting uncomfortable to grow. Dancing to *Hallelujah, Over The Rainbow* and *I Hope You Dance* was uplifting and life changing," says Dixie.

Daly is the 15th of 17 children who recognizes the personal blessings of surrounding herself with like - minded and inspiring humans. If there is one thing Dixie knows, it is true love. Love is the key; love is eternal.

She's especially, proud to be a Nana for 12 beautiful & amazing Grandchildren. And knows that she has the best friends in the world!

First and foremost, she thanks God for giving her the love of her life and her soulmate. She feels like the lucky one to experience so much love, inspiration, and a caring heart from her beloved Ed.

Messages 'From my Heart to Yours', now a journal. *"A Conversation with My Soul"* and *"A Walk to Your Soul,"* are a collection of quotes gifted to me after the passing of my beloved and best friend Ed. These messages have guided me through the most difficult times of my life. The spirit world is more powerful than you will ever imagine. It calms my soul to know there are guardian Angels out there. Miracles will show up in your life in ways you've always dreamed of. Let go of what's holding you back by confirming what is yours, if you really want it. Timing is everything. Once timing aligns with you, everything that is meant to be yours will show up without you expecting it. That is a miracle in itself. One lesson I have learned in life, is that when you make it someone else's responsibility to make you happy, you begin to hold yourself back. The process of living a happy life will be delayed and receiving your gifts that you have been wanting will be prolonged. Therefore, when you put your happiness in your hands you will truly have joy. *Love and appreciate how each and every day has been planned for you and know all you have to do is walk through your purpose with passion.*

Know what you think about, pray about, comes about.

Share *A Conversation with my Soul*, with a friend or family member at:
www.Facebook.com/A Conversation With My Soul and
www.Girlfriendsjourney.com
dixie invites you contact her at:
dixie.aconversationwithmysoul@gmail.com

Thank you for spending time with me on this Journey of read it, write it, journal it . . .
'A Conversation with My Soul' and then a 'Walk to Your Soul'
My hope is that you see the difference in you with messages of hope, faith and love.

Printed in the United States
By Bookmasters

Printed in the United States
By Bookmasters